Life and Opinions

of

Doctor Bop

the

Burnt-Out Prof

and Other Poems

Life and Opinions

of

Doctor Bop

the

Burnt-Out Prof

and Other Poems

E.M. Schorb

Kelsay Books

© 2018 E.M. Schorb. All rights reserved. This material may not be reproduced in any form, published, reprinted, recorded, performed, broadcast, rewritten or redistributed without the explicit permission of E.M. Schorb. All such actions are strictly prohibited by law.

Cover art: E.M. Schorb

ISBN: 978-1-947465-44-2

Kelsay Books
Aldrich Press
www.kelsaybooks.com

For Patricia

Acknowledgments

Grateful acknowledgement is given to the following publications in which some of these poems first appeared:

5 A.M., ArtVilla.com, Blue Unicorn, Chiron Review, Coe Review, Crucible, The Deronda Review, Ginosko Literary Journal, The Kit-Cat Review, Motherbird.com, The Pennsylvania Review, Poetry Super Highway, Private Photo Review, SPRING: The Journal of the E.E. Cummings Society, Tulane Review, Verse, Verse Wisconsin, and *Voices Israel.*

Contents

Part One
Life and Opinions of Doctor Bop

Life and Opinions of Doctor Bop   13

Part Two
Related Poems

Instructions for Life	33
Spine and Spirit	34
Pedantic Piece	36
Ballad of the **B**urnt-**O**ut **P**rof	37
Apologia	40
The Bop Visits Parnassus	42
To the Guardian at the Gate	44
Breathless; or, Overture to Hyperventilation	45

Part Three
Other Poems

What I Did on My Summer Vacation	49
To Menke Katz	51
Oömancery	52
An American Poet on Tour	54
The Road to Nowhere	55
American Paris; or, Undergraduate Days at N.Y.U.	56
Gin Rummies	58
The Woman Who Lives in Me	60
The Diamond Merchant	61

About the Author

Part One

Life and Opinions of Doctor Bop
the
Burnt-Out Prof

Life and Opinions of Doctor Bop
   The Burnt-Out Prof

I. *Veni, Vidi, Vici*

My old man was a *Moishe Kapoyr* if you ever saw one.
This can be proved by the fact that, when I was a kid,
he thought I was a *mazik* and my brother wasn't,
but when we grew up and my brother joined the army
and made a career of it, then he was a *mazik*
and I wasn't, being around the time of which
I speak a college instructor, and I became a *momzer*.
How do you figure? Well, my old man respected
education, but, having very little, was jealous
of those who had it. He claimed fluency in five
languages, all of them Yiddish. "Polymath,"
I said, and he said, "I learned to count on the streets
of New York, making change from what I peddled."
Max was my full brother and, therefore, half Irish too.
Talk about multicultural, we are it. The Irish
side weren't keen on religion, shame to say,
so the old man had his way with us, and I guess
he forgave God for us every Yom Kippur. My mother,
a pliant woman, converted. My brother,
who is the eldest, was born at St. Vincent's
in Greenwich Village, but I was born at Maimonides,
which may suggest a few things I won't go into.
My brother took my mother's Irish name into the army,
where he remains, a Captain now, I think. A *mazik*?
A career man in the army? And not a professor?
My old man was a *Moishe Kapoyr* if you ever saw one.

From such an unpromising background
how do you get started as an academia

nut, and end up having tenure? In those days,
you join the army, of course,
to get the G.I. Bill. 1947:
over a million vets enroll
in colleges under the G.I.
Bill of Rights. Illinois
wins Rose Bowl over U.C.L.A.
45-14, and, in fashion,
the "New Look" comes in,
flat tops, long skirts.
I'm way too young yet,
not even *Bar Mistva'd*,
but eventually I take advantage
of my country's liberal
generosity, for which I thank
the truly great Harry S.,
et. al., and join up.
The Korean armistice was signed
at Panmunjom on July 27, 1953.
Have I got *mazel*! I get the
benefits without the pain.
My old man, who was drafted in the
Great War to end all wars,
sat reading "The Jewish Daily Forward,"
moving from Yiddish to English,
back and forth, back and forth,
learning. He said, "See, you did it again!"
He was pissed because Max,
my truly fabulous big brother,
came home wounded and
deciding to make a career of it,
and I got a vacation in Japan
and Hawaii and came home ready
to "take advantage of the taxpayers,"
like himself, the old *batlan*.
He dies in a conniption fit in '65,

overweight and over Lyndon Johnson's lies,
joining my mother, an angel.

When I was taking my masters at Columbia,
my old man, the meshugge maven, said:
"What do you care for a super goy like Donne?
You said he was a pirate once. I bet
he would come and pull the pale and
take the whole *shtetl* away with him.
And then you say, Dean of St. Paul's—
what would he care for the likes of us?"
"What do *we* care for the likes of us,"
I said, "you even failed in the rag
business, with eighteen relatives to help."
"I had no *mazel*. It's you who's had the luck.
The grants and scholarships you've won!"
"Hard work," I said, "not luck." "Not brains,"
he said. "Your grandfather, he had brains."
"I suppose you mean the Rabbi not the Priest."
"Wise off, wise guy! A sober fur-cutter is better
than a drunken bootlegger." "So why not
cut fur and get as rich as you?" I said.
"I didn't have the eyes for it," he said.
"You got the eyes for anything, and look at you:
John Donne Takes a Holy Crap and Writes a Poem.
Even your drunken Irish bootlegger grandpa
would be royally pissed at that!"

II. *Grooves of Academe*

At the Modern Language Association,
the trees are bending down and going bare, the halls
are getting knee-deep in rusty leaves, and everyone
is pointing a withered finger-stump at everyone else.
The **B**urnt-**O**ut **P**rof is a liberal, but God, a true one.
This is one of the reasons that the Bop is burnt-out:
He finds today an atmosphere of the Inner Circle

of the old Kremlin, where "normal" means what anyone desires.
It is like the old days when Political Correctness meant
the Party line of the week, sometimes posted in "Pravda,"
or telephoned to London, Paris, and New York, to
prepare for diplomatic divagations, on the weekend.
This week sexy is sexist, so I don't know how to explain myself.
I can tell you, It's getting tough to say much of anything.
1736: Patrick Henry was born. That was also the year
that Fahrenheit died and Hogarth produced his "Good Samaritan."
None of these things seem to have had much "impact,"
(now there's a word that I would ban) and,
while I wend my way through this historic traffic,
toward an historic college that no longer
recognizes history as a legitimate subject,
I notice that the leaves are down and tumbling
in the wind along the road to higher learning.

Taking by storm the bastions of conditioned reflex,
I sat down to reflect on the mystery of life,
but found myself instead considering whether to refinance
the old adobe of my dreams, now that the rates were lower.
The school had found my house for me—the school's my mother.
I had a real mother but the school's a better mother: Magna Mater.
(One keeps thinking of Magna-Matergate, but so far so good.)
Along the treelined drives . . . etc. lateral thinking impinged,
and before you could say, "Peter Piper picked,"
I considered the deconstruction, not of all the texts in the school,
but of the school itself, slate by slate and brick by brick.
I could start at the highest point—was it the flagpole
or the tower clock? In an *augenblick* a Hamlet's confusion befell
   me.
The other day I asked our professor of Medieval History a question
only to learn that her expertness (or "tise") was restricted
to the period between when Constantine reigned alone
and St. Vladimir became prince of Kiev, with everything else
outside her field. *To our professor of Medieval History
the rest of life is a mystery;* no generalist, she. Life is not her field.

The middle-aged scribes on the staff correct the English
of the professors and fund-raisers alike, that no embarrassment
befalls these ivied halls. They are made of substantial stuff,
the staff, the grade- and high-school grads of yesteryear,
like Hemingway and Faulkner.
1899: John Dewey, "School and Society." *Tunc pro nunc.*
Another new building is going up on the green.

I am Anarchus, King of Academe,
tenured to bring chaos to your campus.
I can say any goddam irresponsible frigging thing.
I am a regular irrepressible intellectual Wild Bull of the Pampas.

I'll be your peripatetic in the feeble rain.
I'll corrupt you with my Socratic questions.
When God commanded Hosea to associate with a whore,
Wasn't that a command against the Decalogue?

Aquinas said No, because in so commanding,
the whore became Hosea's wife.
Everything fits, you see, Pangloss-like.
Just when we think something has gone wrong

it has come up right. How sure are you
of anything? The skeleton of Cro-Magnon man
was found in France in 1868.
Who moved it, and from where? And why?

In 1871, Adolf Nordenskjöld explored the interior
of Greenland. There was no there there, as Gert Stein put it,
but he did it because it was there, as Sir Edmund Hillary put it.
Hath the rain a father? Where is love?

Principles are never provable
in the order which they substantiate,
they are evident and intuitively given.
That should be some help with regard to love.

In 1805, Hosea Ballou wrote "A Treatise on Atonement."
Mobile perpetuum. You who are young
will soon be old and walking with the young.
The "Treatise" will await you in "La morgue littéraire."

Young Sirs, Bruno proclaimed the spatial and material infinity of
    the world.
Ladies, Descartes attributed positive infinity only to God.
Newton was cautious. Einstein certain. Planck confusing.
Maybe we should just make love and listen to the music of the
    rain.

When Chips left the Old School he wore its tie
and was carried out with his Wellingtons on.
But no way Doctor Bop, the burnt-out prof.
Things definitely ain't what they used to be.
Bop gets to retire on something like a 401(k);
but not yet, as St. Augustine put it, not quite yet;
I'm not ready for retired sainthood yet!
The syllogisms from which Aristotle deduced the valid
are not complete. In American institutions
we fail upward to glory, and I expect
to be the mad head of the English Department before
I wallop my last tennis ball to cardiac arrest,
or do my last imitation of Johnny Weissmuller.
"Thanatopsis" is *not* my favorite poem.

III. *A Speed of Semesters*

"Coleridge did dope," she said.
"So one day, when he was socked out,
dreaming up this poem about Xanadu,
along came this person from Porlock
on some business and shook him out of it.

After about an hour he couldn't remember
anything but the first part of the poem.
Has that ever happened to you? I mean,
that poem of yours in the 'American Scholar,'
seems unfinished, you know?" A very
finished young lady, and this is what
I get! I give them some *Biographia
Literaria*, in a vague hope . . .
"Fancy and imagination!" I roar,
and point to someone else.
"Fancy is only memory and produces
only a sensational product.
Imagination transcends time and
makes contact with higher reality."
Something occurs to me: "No,
I don't *do* dope, and the poem
is finished because it says
what it started out to say
in the way it started out to say it."
"I only meant, have you ever been
interrupted when you were writing
a poem, so that the unfinished part
transcends and makes contact with
a higher reality, like that one
in the 'American Scholar'?"
And suddenly I realized how very quick
she was, and nice, and pretty too.

The Greeks measured Earth by its shadow on the moon.
I measure it by travel, which always brings you home;
therefore, Thomas Wolfe was wrong. Good news, though—
Pascal was probably right. I'd be willing to bet on it.
I had an uncle in the numbers racket, himself a gambler.
Thoreau said, Time is a stream I go fishing in.
Ford said, History is the bunk. Sumerian writing
done on clay tablets, shows about 2000 pictographic signs.
The moon is a bad woman because she is very romantic.

We all know the trouble that can get you into. I
am romantic tonight. How many leaves lay scattered?
I guess millions, and I have a study that agrees with me.
When you pay for a study, you get what you pay for.
Therefore, all studies are romantic and have a dark side.
Humankind pays for everything it gets. Theodora,
the Byzantine empress, died in 548, one of a kind.
Her death was a big relief to some of her subjects.
Five years later disastrous earthquakes shook the entire world.
I offer no comment, but think about it.
The house I live in was built much later. I leave the
actual count to you. Do not use a calculator.
The first water-driven mechanical clock was
constructed in Peking in 1090, the wrist watch
around the turn of the twentieth century.
I've got a digital that I can read in the dark.
I can also read the chained and sailing moon from here.
Shaw said, give him a slate and a piece of chalk
and he'd give you the wrong answer in under five minutes.
A journey of a thousand miles begins with one step,
so I lift my gouty foot and lean forward. Good counting!

"Look at you," said Müller,
who taught psychology,
and later committed suicide
when implicated in war crimes.
A vegetarian, he picked
at his salad and eyed me
with distaste. I was drinking
a whiskey sour. "You have ashes
down the front of your shirt.
It is a dirty habit, smoking.
And I see you always drinking
in that cocktail bar by the
lake. You must take better
care of yourself, my friend."

"Worry is what kills you.
I grade papers there. It's
very pleasant—a beautiful view,
even in winter, when the lake looks
like a bowl of liquid iron. You
know, in 1496, Romano Pane,
a monk who accompanied Columbus,
became the first person to
describe the tobacco plant
to the old world. Tobacco
was brought from America
to Spain in 1555. In 1560,
the tobacco plant was imported
to Western Europe by Jean Nicot;
hence, nicotine. It brought
pleasure and pain, as all things do."

"How do you know such things
—dates like that, I mean?"

"I look them up. They're
comforting, definite.
Very little is." "You appear
detached." "Not detached.
Perhaps transcendent. Sir
John Hawkins introduced
tobacco into England
in 1565. That was the same
year that pencils began
to be manufactured there.
Also, Sir Thomas Gresham
founded the Royal Exchange
in London, same year. And
the Knights of St. John,
under Jean de La Valette,
defended Malta from the Turks.
The Turkish siege was broken with
the arrival of Spanish troops."

"What's the difference?"
"Exactly! Erskine Caldwell
published Tobacco Road in 1932.
Jack Kirkland's play version
of TR opened to a long run
in New York in '33. But
at the end of the century
I have to go outside to smoke,
and the autumn wind blows
the ashes all over me."

"I should like my ashes
to be scattered over the lake,"
Müller said. I lit another
cigarette, watched the smoke
scurry off in puffs and strands.
"I'll see to it," I said.

The true task is to trace the phenomena
back to the hidden Logos, i.e., spirit and reason.
The two ways of looking at this, though,
cause trouble. Is God in or not in Nature?
Have the monotheists got hold of the right end
of the stick, or have the Hindus and Buddhists;
are the Pantheists right or are the Christians?
But infinity does not exclude its middle.
God, however, can make an infinity.
1941: Étienne Gilson: *God and Philosophy*;
Reinhold Niebuhr: *The Nature and Destiny
of Man;* and Bergson died. I played war
at my grandmother's house in New Jersey.
On July 16th, the first atomic bomb
was detonated near Alamogordo, N.M.
On August 6th and August 9th, the U.S.
dropped atomic bombs on Hiroshima and
Nagasaki. On her back porch, my grandmother

told me that no one would be able to live
in those cities for a hundred years to come.
Nine years later I was there. The thousand-
year Reich had lasted twelve years. The Logos
is deeply hidden. Near the end of the war, bebop
came in. People would sit along a bar and move
their heads side to side, idiotically. The modern
school believes we must assert nothing
but "essence" and "meaning." I read
Kon-Tiki on the ship that took me to Japan.
Heyerdahl believed in the probable colonization
of Polynesia from South America around 1100.
I remember reading and looking at the water,
reading and looking at the water.

You know how it is when you feel sure
of something, maybe a date,
or a fact of some kind,
and then you find out that you were wrong
and you feel like your brain's
turned into camel-shit and got
spread across the Sahara, well,
I made a bet with a faculty member
that I knew the exact date,
there and then, and where and when,
of the invention of the thermometer.
The faculty member teaches pre-
med, and we were at a table
in the school cafeteria. She shoves
a five-dollar bill out, and triumphantly
I assert: Santorio Santorio
measured human temperature
with a thermometer in Italy in 1628.
"But he did not *invent* the thermometer,"
she says, and picks up her five-spot.
"Fahrenheit initiated mercury as a heat-
measuring medium. R.A.F. de Réaumur

used alcohol. And then there was
Celsius." I had got a hold of
the wrong end of the thermometer, and
out dropped my brain from one camel's ass,
stepped on by the big hoofs of the next, and
dragged across the desert by the caravan.
I should have learned a long time ago
about never being entirely certain
of anything. God may not play tricks,
as Einstein insisted, but life does,
with a little help from human
arrogance, of the kind I displayed,
and the endless capacity of the
human mind to misconceive and
misperceive, and the plain simple
strangeness of life itself, and
that must be the case. Maybe.

Is the peripatetic part of the meaningless goo
this autumn that is being trounced by the rain,
one with the fallen beaten leaves? Camus
and Sartre would insist on seizing pain
by the throat and giving it a throttle,
being that we are all alone with it
like a drunk in a rented room with a bottle
and not a 'toon in which to spit.
Up to us, they would say, to do something about it,
be a "Renegade" or find "No Exit"
or become one's own kind of Mister Fix-it,
but of its ultimate use, I doubt it,
doubt we can do it alone,
doubt it to the bone.

IV. *Sabbatical*

If the word of the creator is itself creation,
as in "Let there be light," and since the birth of the world
is linked to the birth of the word, isn't it so
that the essence of language is in the spirit, the Logos?
Then the rants of the mad and the speakers in tongues
are holy and creative rants and speakers and poets
of portmanteau words and nonsense rhymes are makers
of the solidly new and true, and are meant to be translated,
paraphrased or whatever can be done to understand them.

I have the distinct honor to know several people who are mad
and who do not mind sitting across from me and spewing
out their hearts and minds. 1533: First lunatic asylums
(without medical attention). Freud taught us to listen.
But we know now that schizophrenia is a kind of brain rot,
an actual physical condition, and is already treatable
with chemicals. Listening would not have helped the insane;
but it might have helped the sane, if they were able to interpret,
for the words were palpable. My friend shouts, "Mother ate me!"
and I get his drift; "Father buried me alive," and I dig.
"It isn't the dream but the words you use to describe the dream,"
wrote Freud in *The Interpretation of Dreams* in 1900. Blake:
"The lost traveller's dream under the hill."
I myself dreamed of being in a long queue behind Princess Di.
I suppose everything is in there—royalty, sex, and death.

Shall we become public figures,
sharing the thin metaphorical blood of fraternity?
Shall we be the Family of Man (and Woman, of course)
or shall we be a flesh and blood family
at war and peace with ourselves and the State?
We can't love what we don't know.
We are asked to stretch fraternity's blood
until we become anemic, pale pretenders
to emotion, vampires of passion.

It is paradox. If I keep my brother,
I become his keeper, and he the kept,
not free, not equal, not his own.
And if I turn in surrender to my vision,
I must master others, keep my brother,
and I must rob him of his vision
as my vision dominates his, oh Abel!
If I lead, he must follow whither.
He must wither following. He must say:
But where is my vision of home and hearth,
where wife, where blood-rich children?
If his children are my children,
where are his children?
Is my avuncular blood as rich
as that of his and his wife's?
Fraternity's blood runs thin and thinner
until it is water and we are bound by water
alone, ice water, not the sticky rich blood
of consanguinity, the stuff of passionate caring.
Would a watery world be better?
Remember how many vows have been broken.
Remember the blood oaths of children,
your blood-brothers and -sisters who are
gone with your childhood, how each
cut a finger enough for blood and
stuck them together, and how gone
is an event where you can only recall
what you did and not with whom
in a dark corner of the Kabbalah.

If you stop to think about it,
the twenty-six point-whatever miles back from Marathon
never did anyone much good. I used to believe
what Santayana said, but the generations are too far apart,
and one lost one will put us back to square one again.
I live near the second largest artificial lake in America,
and all my less sedentary colleagues are boaters and campers,

and they are always trying to get me into a boat or a camp;
but when I was young I spent a lot of time on ships and boats
and beaches, like Ulysses, and I tell them a cocktail bar
is the most civilized place on Earth. You go in and sit down
and order a Gibson, light up, and wait
for some intelligent conversation to break out.
Of course you are costing the public a fortune because none of this
is good for your health—it obviously killed George Burns, at
age 100, before his time—but I'm with the Sun King and his
"Après moi, le déluge." I'm a sort of professorial sociopath,
I guess, always thinking that if I have one life to live
I'll live it my way—so I go over and plug "My Way" on the jukebox.
I hope I'm a bad influence on my students, just like Sinatra and
Socrates, and I intend to spend the rest of my life as a Clairol
    blond,
asking plenty of pointless questions of the vacuous sky.

1913: The Armory Show introduced cubism to New York.
The Nude Descending a Staircase left us exhausted.
Her energy was obvious but we were drained by her élan.
In 1918 we lay there smoking and wondering who had been super.
In 1929 we lost faith in money, in '42 safety.
And now the last securities and guarantees have disappeared.
Living with the bomb has made tragedy impossible.
"Dr. Strangelove, or How I Learned to Live with the Bomb,"
is a comedy. No deliberate war was possible,
because leaders were targeted and are cowardly,
but accidents are inevitable. The little girl picking flowers
in Lyndon Johnson's ad, 1964: then his big lie.
The cup of our political faith became a sieve, too. Johnson had
done for American politics what Planck did for particle stability.
I can only understand myself in my hereness now.
I step forth in fact but my whereness is a mystery.
I wait outside the seasons for a cue.

V. *Commence Fire!*

The question of the truly real
has metastasized in me,
like the spread ambition of a runner
whose toes are fat with it.
The central emotional tumor
of desire to know what is behind the
screen of existence is devouring me.
It has reached Faustian proportions with
increasing age. Sometimes I must dull
the ache of it with booze and music,
sometimes with what comedy I can find
in the happenings around me. Calling
life a game is a withdrawal symptom,
a relief from the wracked nerves of wonder,
by which I have been attended since I was a child:
wonder and wondering. I could get sick
with it, when young, and did. The doctors
wondered too, and my poor father paid them.
It's a kind of ontological hypochondria,
which has turned me, slowly, but ever so surely,
into an intellectual valetudinarian.

A poem is a posit, an assertion, an act,
and in action we forget fear: respite
in creation, the maker takes a stand, in making,
but is it a stand no better than gimmick-makers make?
Well, poetry possesses the virtue of being a record,
at least, and you can date a poem, if you wish,
thus giving it the merit of a worldly fact
contained in a system of time, which, admittedly,
is a system which is perhaps pseudo-fact itself,
or will become so as matter completes its withdrawal
upon itself to revisit its beginnings in a black hole in space;
and yet, until then, something like a fact,
a fact in the sense that Sherlock Holmes is almost real
and lives in Baker Street in a fictional series

in a real world that may exist only in a dream
that is being dreamed elsewhere, perhaps—dare I say—
by Yahweh; and so poetry becomes an actual little stab
and, poets hope, rip in the black sheet
that covers the deserted, haunted mansion.

If you expect happiness you get misery,
but just when you learn to live with misery
the cat comes back and wants to be fed,
so you feed the cat and that makes you feel better.
Expressionists always bring the problem of death forward,
demanding an "authentic death," an act of dying
that is peculiarly one's own (as in Rilke:
Notebooks of Malte Laurids Brigge).
What good does it do to say that you are an expressionist
or for that matter an existentialist, or any ist?
"Poetry is of graver import than history," said Aristotle.
Why? Because good poetry doesn't know what to do, doesn't try
to tell anyone else what to do. True, Yeats made a system,
and Blake before him, but they did it for scaffolding,
to shoot darts of insight from and toward, not
to believe in, not to insist upon—monkeybars
to climb in and to swing through. If you expect
happiness you get misery, but then the cat will come home,
expecting to be fed, and that makes you feel much better.

2300 folding chairs on the lawn,
relatives with an actuarial average
of 30 years left in them,
fathers less, mothers more,
and grandmothers more than ever
(I hasten to add, non-smokers
more than anyone), myself
hot on a warm June day:
commencement socializing:
1888: Lover's Leap and
Hold-Me-Tight buggies: today
expensive sports cars

for the kids, up to limousines for
the relatives. The campus
is crowded with vehicles, gleaming
colors abound: chauffeurs
stand in clusters of uniforms, smoking.
I envy them. Grads with an actuarial life
of 50 years ahead of them,
maybe 60, sweat with heat
and excitement, caps and gowns,
and in anticipation of booze,
dancing, prancing, and romancing
tonight: but first, ROTC
commissioning, Baccalaureate
Service, Supper with the
school President and his wife
(parents and their students are urged
to remain on campus for Supper),
Open Houses, faculty and staff
homes, a concert by the college choir,
a Jazz ensemble. There won't be a
hotel or motel room empty
for a radius of 50 miles.
I scan young faces in the hope
that some of them know
the difference between fancy
and the imagination,
between a Baccalaureate and
a Bacchanalia, between
an apposable behind and
a prehensile tail, etc.
Orator fit, poeta nascitur.
Poeta nascitur, non fit.
I'm halfway into the wrong racket.
I'm quitting school to write:
retiring from the fray,
I'll go to Innisfree.
Bon voyage, and
vaya con Dios, my darlings!

Part Two

Related Poems

Instructions for Life

Argonauts looking for the Holy Grail, are we, or the Golden Fleece?
An adventure is a game too. 549: in the Neo-Persian Empire music, dancing, chess, and hunting, are cultivated; humankind being busy. The importance of every man, woman, and child was recognized by the Treaty with God, a dateless, timeless document.
The importance of every man, woman, and child was recognized again
by the Treaty with Sartre, circa 1950. Know that it's a do-it yourself
world, and then you can begin to take yourself seriously in your quest.

Spine and Spirit

to my cat, Vicki

All I care about is vertebrates.
I can't help it, I'm made that way.
It's true that invertebrates kept on evolving
after vertebrates arrived, but who cares.
There are slinky vertebrates, though,
but I won't mention any names—a job's a job.
In Western religious tradition
the spiritual is identified with a purposive order.
In 540 the Empress Theodora introduced long white dresses,
purple cloaks, gold embroidery, tiaras, and pointed shoes.
In 542 the plague of Constantinople,
imported by rats from Egypt and Syria,
spread all over Europe. By 547, the plague,
medically described by Gildas, reached Britain.
Cause and effect? The slinkiest person I ever saw
I saw at Minsky's burlesque in Newark when I was sixteen.
I think Senator Long may have met her there, backstage.
Well, different features of the human spirit have been stressed
in different idealist systems: knowing and the
attributes of thought, perceiving with retrospective memory
and creative imagination, willing and the tumults of striving,
purpose and the organization it gives to activity,
each have been taken as the essential activity or
distinguishing mark of spirit. Blaze Starr.
Marie Curie: 1911 Nobel Prize for Chemistry.
Also, British Official Secrets Act becomes law.
All of these things are connected to vertebrates,
even as the path of evolution leads us downward
toward television. Primacy of spirit
may be taken as a sense of mastery,
and mean the spirit's omnipotence in the world,

and in the individual the dominance of soul over body.
The notochord cannot replace the vertebrae,
so the shark is a soul-less hunger. The case
could be made. What about extraterrestrials, though?
Beings made of gas? Well, the backbone was made of gas,
i.e., Senator Long's backbone and Blaze Starr's slinky
spine: and imagine those two vertebrates going at it.
And what about Madame Curie's curious chemistry?
I must agree with Pascal. I must assert the primacy of spirit
and to hell with the backbone; but that would mean
that one must have some backbone in order to assert
the primacy of spirit, a backbreaking thought.

Pedantic Piece

If you have no verbs,
you must *do* everything;
but, really, you must not:
not, for instance, *do* dope.

May I lend you a verb?
Do you wish to *use,*
misuse, abuse, to
inhale, inject, ingest,
or do you wish to *do,* dope?

Well, don't; don't *do* dope.
Do do something else.

Ballad of the Burnt-Out Prof

> *...Something... eternally gained...*
> *for the universe...*
> —William James

Old Duracell, old Mazda-man
You've got to keep the light—
It's growing dim inside you
but that's no time to hide you—
there's just a chance you might
say something shedding light.

Old Candle-wick, old Burnt-Out Prof,
(who calls himself the Bop)
old hairy ears and snout,
Tochis afn tish!
you gouty worn-out lout—
oh, call yourself a name, old cuss—
because you weren't the best,
and yet you know it doesn't matter,
no, not in the least.

Old geeze, don't lose your grip,
Don't fall and break your hip—
You've got to keep the light, baldspot,
You've got to keep the light,
because there's just a chance
if you keep the light, old souse,
if you keep the light,
there's still a chance, though mad,
that there's something left to add.

You've got to keep the light, old piles,
You've got to keep the light.
You know you've been a dog,

oh, you've acted like a *trayf* old hog,
but somehow in your life
you've had a loving wife,
so there must be something good about you,
you lousy lucky lout you—
all I ask of you, old candle,
is just to keep the Godblessed light,
and show a flash of pluck, old duck,
and with a bit of luck
you might come up with something
worthy of the world that you've surveyed.

You've been around so long now
you've got to hold some light,
whether hell or heaven
is waiting with its leaven
to galvanize you new again
for better or for worse,
old man of steel, who once pumped iron,
don't listen to that deathly siren,
you've got to keep the light a while,
you've got to keep that gap-toothed smile,
you've got to keep the light alive
inside your horrible old hide,
because you still might do a thing
that's worthy of its doing,
you've got to keep the light, old pipe,
you've got to keep the light.

You've written many a poem, old bard,
and published many too,
but I've got news for you, old prof,

I've got news for you—
you haven't any right, old cough,
not to keep the light.
You don't get off like that, old shakes
fall off the roof like that—
there's plenty time to die, old guy,
plenty time to die,
so keep on pumping light, old Bop,
pumping students light!

Apologia

I've been told that I don't take life seriously enough,
or, conversely, that I make a serious effort at skimming its surface,
that I'm content to be a generalist, the kind of roller-blader
who shies at summersaults, the runner who runs the marathon
to see the crowd, the kind of drinker who tries not to get drunk,
the kind of no-good clod who would call an activist an officious-
    intermeddler
or, worse, a busybody, the kind of not-engaged guy who won't
march, who looks out at the world through stained glass eyes
as if it were his 57th visit to the Rocky Horror Picture Show.

Well, I can't account for what others may think, but,
my apologia is, that, with the rest of the variously displaced
    modern world,
I've experienced a surfeit leading to confusion, have become
    ideophobic,
even a doubter of doubts, who wonders at times if the old oak tree
    is its phenomenology,
or its rugged trunk and russet autumn leaves that lend it its poetic
    dignity
and pictorial poetry: for I think that our gravest thoughts are
    rooted
in buried and forgotten or half-forgotten metaphor, as in "the sun
    rises,"
rather than "the Earth goes down," and that the corrupt text of our
    political language
is too obvious a deconstructivist challenge for an intelligent child.

Donne couldn't have imagined that his hated "New Philosophy"
    would bring us to a world of ephemerons and quarks,
nor that, scarcely out of the dark ages, his renaissance would lead
    to the

evils of the century we have just nearly struggled through. No thanks, been there, done that, it's a lost cause.

The stately metaphorical summertime virescence of the next century awaits us. Sure it does.

The Bop Visits Parnassus

Students, ladies and gents,
8000 feet below Parnassus
Delphi told me the road.
I decided to go to the top,
and visit with great Apollo.
    On the way up, I stopped
    to see the Castalian fountain
    where the Pythian games were held,
    and there I met piping Pan,
    whose crazy legs were crossed
    as he played upon a rock,
    and asked him where I could find
    Dionysus today, for I had
    an ungodly need of a mead
    from climbing, and was told:
    "He's rather high today."
Silenus sat with Pan,
who was surrounded by Bacchae.
"He isn't Bacchus, you know.
He goes his own way," said Silenus.
"I quite understand," I replied,
and climbed to the very top.
    There I discovered the Great One.
    Yes, great Apollo smiled on me.
    "I am Apollo, son of Zeus,
    and I welcome you here to Parnassus,"
    he said. "I am god of music,
    poetry, and healing," he went on,
    "and represent light and the sun."
"Thank you for your kind welcome,"
I replied. "I've come a pilgrimage
for healing by music and poems.
Please, grant me my wish, great god,
and restore me to my old health,

for my mind is weary with facts."
Oh his poems and sweet music restored me,
and I vowed that, upon my return,
I should tell of his healing power,
his beauty, his radiant smile,
his sun-bronzed body, and, oh,
praise therapeutic Apollo,
so superior to healers below.

To the Guardian at the Gate

Happiness over my shoulder is a cloud of ink.
Destroyed again by the world last Monday, I
can no longer agree that the fault is mine
and not in my stars. When the fault is yours
you can do something about it, take a course
in constancy or begin once again to build up your muscles.
You have to believe you can make life work on your own.
You have to believe in something, no matter how weird,
something to cure ill. Nicholas Prevost of Tours,
1098: "Antidotarum," a collection of 2650
medical prescriptions from Salerno. In the modern age,
the being and existence of things are determined
through comprehensibility, ascertained by us,
which amounts to saying that if we don't understand it,
it isn't. So the bad stuff isn't there because
I don't understand why it has to be. Happiness
over my shoulder turns back into a silken cloud,
which is either a way of saying that life
is what we make of it or that we are mad
as two unpaid fighting cocks with razor spurs
ripping ourselves apart for nothing but a bit of corn.
But if life is good, why are the feathers always flying?
To end on a high note, try hypnotizing yourself into hope.
Get that cloud of ink back down onto paper where it belongs,
and don't look back, for God's sake, don't look back!

Breathless; or, Overture to Hyperventilation

You know how it is with daily life,
never enough time to do anything,
and especially never enough time for making love:
early rising rushing to exhaustion earning a living,
no food for thought, and especially no stimulating Ovidian oysters.
Lunch in a bag, maybe. Make the bag big enough for your head
and save it, you'll need it. This is the overture to hyperventilation,
which leads to the loss of carbon dioxide from the blood.
1944: Lewis Mumford: "The Condition of Man," who
is understood as being thrown out of a state of security
and into a dark night of suffering where the world is lost to him
and back upon himself and forced to reflection, self-awakening,
and finally to authentic, breathless being,
as he climbs the stairs to his bedroom at night,
where his beloved awaits him like an opening rose.
471: Aeschylus introduces a second actor.
But Arthur Miller says tragedy is impossible in our time.
Only drama. It's dramatic to lose your breath.
When you get it back, you laugh because you were so silly,
and life returns to comedy. Mostly, life is comedy with gravitas,
universal, intergalactic comedy, but the mice on the mudball
are forced to take it seriously. Ah breathless, breathless!
Kierkegaard possessed a certain sense of security,
but his way would mean church and no love on Sunday morning,
the only remaining opportunity. Working people need a chance.
The Spanish close shop and take a two-hour siesta afternoons
but I wager don't get much more than a catnap out of it.
And, Venus, when you rise naked before me on the half-shell
of our conch-colored couch, my heart goes into rapid fire,
for the time has finally come, as it will to the good and the patient,
and I gulp for breath at sight of you and breathe until I'm
    breathless.

Part Three

Other Poems

What I Did on My Summer Vacation

This summer I flew to Trieste
to visit with Joyce, then
journeyed to Prague to find Kafka.
In Hamburg I had many a few
steins of beer with Thomas Wolfe,
and, because the Literary
Travel Agency rushed my itinerary,
soon found myself chugging through
the Chunnel and into Poets'
Corner at Westminster Abbey,
where I ran into a raging Dylan
Thomas. He hated the States
but loved Third Avenue, so
he said he would help me
paint London red, white, and blue.
Next morning we had vanilla
ice-cream in our beer
for our health's sake. Later
that afternoon Caitlin kicked
the stilts out from under his house,
so I thought it was time to leave
them there, under milk wood,
and get on to the relative peace
and quiet of Ireland, where I
visited with Pat Kavanagh,
who had come to regard comedy
as the "ultimate sophistication,"
which ordinary people, "do not
understand and therefore fear."
Pat believed that in tragedy
"there is always something of a
lie... comedy is the abundance

of life," etc., but I had to leave
him there, laughing at himself,
and life in general, and catch
the train on to Heathrow.
I landed in New York, where I
was met by Walt Whitman, who
was holding up a dishevelled Eddie
Poe, who greeted me with a wet kiss.
I got a manly hug from Walt. Then
I flew back down to Asheville to
present Wolfe's hometown with
his latest, *You Can't Go Home
Again,* which he gave me in
manuscript (much edited
by Max Perkins) and then drove
back to the College by the Lake
—and here I am, grading papers.

To Menke Katz

O
Menke,
with your sweet
mandolin and
thick-accented song,
your poetry of
burning villages and
brave forays beyond the pale,
of coming to America
and golden Lower East Side streets,
of the secret laughter at the center
of the most Holy Kabbalah, O Menke,
for you, dead at nearly ninety, I write
this Katzian sonnet. The body sleeps to free the soul.

Oömancery

Oömancery is the magic of the universe
popping out of an egg.
I don't see why the universe should not
pop out of an egg, or into one.

I read with my morning coffee,
in the *New York Times,*
of a new theory of physics,
providing for the possible

existence of multiple universes,
unknown to one another.
I don't see why there should not be
multiple universes.

I am so intrigued by the notion
that I fail to notice
that there are innumerable presences
in my house and that they are

attempting to tell me something.
I catch myself up and listen
but can only hear suggestions:
Mister Breeze, Mistress Boardcreak,

Master Bark, and little Miss Sigh,
speaking ineffably to me. Zounds!
Are their voices coming from my holy egg?
The light on the walls is

filled with dancing wings.
My egg is beautiful,
but not too beautiful to eat.
I swallow the soft-boiled universe

whole, and wash it down with coffee.
Now I am in one and have one in me.
The theory of multiple universes
has been proven to my satisfaction.

An American Poet on Tour

I suppose it was somewhat
like this in the Hellenistic
age, when you could go in every direction
from Athens and still be a Greek
and I suppose it was somewhat
like this in the Roman
when all roads led away
and back to Rome and
I suppose it was somewhat
like this when the sun never set
on the old British Empire,
so this is what we Americans get
for being the so-called superpower.

I have been thinking these thoughts
on a plane for an hour—
how every place I land
seems like the place I just left—
and now I think I understand
just what Gert Stein meant
when she said what she said
in her odd and idiosyncratic bent
about the place she had come from
where there was no there there.
Anyway this morning wherever I am
the weather seems fair
and maybe they'll like me here.

The Road to Nowhere

Winged and hovering overhead
Victory awaits my confession of defeat
snatched from itself by lost control.
Some tell us to be ourselves
but if ourselves contain
the seed of the enigma tree
that flowers black and hangs down so,
what should we do, *wee* ones before its cloud
of multitudinous, oily leaves?

It's not on that highway
but off into the field
for pastures of plenty,
our idea of virtue and beauty,
the apparitions row on row
of rich successes reaped
for services not rendered,
not endured.

American Paris; or, Undergraduate Days at N.Y.U.

Seeing in my mind now those winding, those twisting and
    turning, those populace
        and spiraling streets,
the carts full of produce and the sausages hanging from
    hooks in shop windows
        along MacDougal Street, the

bread, full of crunch, and tasting again the tang on my lips,
    purpled with wine,
        seeing myself strolling
the Washington Square where Henry of James fame dreamed
    his intransigent
        heiress, her hair

in a hurting knot, and sitting at the fountain, or on the
    rails at the foot of the park
        near my new,
old school, ah, seeing the paintings outdoors on display at the
    rails, as if Manet and
        Monet, the pre-

and the post- of impressionists, the Fauves and the Cubists,
    Picasso,
        and splattering Pollock,
were hawking their wares, remembering wandering from where
    the flowering boppers would follow me
        to espresso cafes

to the beat of a bongo or the twang of a Bob Dylan song,
    and of course remembering the
        first loves of youth,

difficult, daring, darling, oh, and, drawing back from the
    darkening window of then,
        where the street corner

lamp glowed like a crystal ball with no knowledge of anything
    but my dream
        of a fabulous future,
I think lovingly of the Village of the Sixties as my own
    American Paris
        in the fargone time of my innocence.

Gin Rummies

To find a friend one must close one eye.
To keep him—two.
                —Norman Douglas

for Rodney Formon

Friday nights, a fry-cook,
arms scarred by sizzling fat,
Rodney bangs on my door.
We like to drink together,
shoot the breeze, and laugh.
Drunk enough, we sing!
It's karaoke with CDs scattered
on the table, improvisational
shandygaffs and combinations
you can't enjoy with your relations.

It's good to have a drinking buddy.
I've used up two already—
one who fell down a flight of stairs
and one, who was much older,
who died of his warrior life.
But now I've got Rodney,
who is very different from the others.

The other two were quite and somewhat
intellectual, and where the one
could talk history or science, art,
music, or just about any subject
in just about any language and come back,
being polyglot, and polymath,
even polymorphic, after hooch;
the other was a man of action,
a war hero with many medals
tucked away in drawers locked

by indifference, but still would tell of
weapons, arms and the man, and such
with fervor—my Heraclitus—
and also with disgust, with
fatalism, believing nothing
changes in man's fighting nature,
disposed to think the worst;
but enthusiastic over chess,
which he played in earnest
as if he were at war again.

But Rodney is another sort:
He knows I write but will not read
a word I write, nor much else either,
but likes the Internet so much
he slides crabwise in thought,
toward what depth of cyberspace
I often cannot fathom until *zing*
I see it for myself, or am I drunk?

I see with Rodney that the other two,
complimented first my young and then
my middle-aged delusions
of a deeper self-knowledge
than available to most. Yes, Rodney
shows me to myself, or shows me
to my youthful ghosts, as ego-fed,
but did and does this unintentionally,
whose wonderful indifference makes me shrink
like a cock in the cold, and chug my drink.

The Woman Who Lives in Me

The woman who lives in me, wet with desire,
can never give me up, no matter what I do.
For a fortnight I ignore her, but she's there
waiting pantyless and panting near my heart
that pumps for her and fills my member up.
She is my muse of sex, my succubus,
my sensuality so I can paint a nude.
When I look at winter her warmth flows into me,
and when I march, she is my vivandière.
She gets the outer ones to bear the children of my loins
so she can keep her figure that my mouth may water.
When I harass her with my sex, I hear her laughter.
Oh she needs no foreplay and she never sues.
She keeps my age so she can die with me.

The Diamond Merchant

A diamond is forever.
—B. J. Kidd

The buoys of memory have faint bells, noticed in the night.
I have left these chiming seamarks for the time of my return.
They ring out there, but faintly, so faintly I can hardly hear.
I think they want me to remember the severances of the soul,
if soul is more than mere electric tissue. If Death is king
and I do not reclaim what I have jettisoned, it goes to him.
I do not want the king to have my life. Therefore, each night at
    sea,
I must set out to find the ringing buoys and haul aboard
the lagan realities, for now my aging body, my emotional mal de
    mer,
lend renewed reality to the cold, damp camps. One numbered
    friend
should wear a wedding ring, another was engaged, and yet a third,
below and silent, had eyes like Tavernier blue diamonds set in Fabergé
eggshell by the master. I cannot put a name to the smiling face I
    see,
but she existed, who is now the faint dream of a denouement.

Shalom alekhem   Shalom alekhem

So now I sail all night to find them and their symbols, to
connect with them whatever seems appropriate, their rings,
their eyes, their ways: but not alone to find the persons
but to find the meanings of the persons to myself, the electric
mind, before the king should claim them from my life.

About the Author

E.M. Schorb is a prize-winning poet and novelist. His most recent poetry collection is *Emanations from the Penumbra*, Hill House New York. Earlier, his *Murderer's Day,* was awarded the Verna Emery Poetry Prize and published by Purdue University Press, and a prior collection, *Time and Fevers*, was the recipient of the Writer's Digest International Self-Published Award for Poetry and also an Eric Hoffer Award.

Other works include *50 Poems,* Hill House New York; *Reflections in a Doubtful I,* White Violet Press; *The Journey and Related Poems,* Aldrich Press; *Words in Passing,* The New Formalist Press; *The Ideologues and Other Retrospective Poems,* Aldrich Press; *Eclectica Americana,* Hill House New York; *Manhattan Spleen,* Aldrich Press; *Last Exit to East Hampton,* Kelsay Books; and *The Poor Boy,* Dragon's Teeth Press, Living Poets Series. The title poem, "The Poor Boy," was awarded the International Keats Poetry Prize by London Literary Editions, Ltd., judged by Howard Sergeant.

Schorb's novel, *Paradise Square,* received the Grand Prize for Fiction from the International eBook Award Foundation at the Frankfurt Book Fair. *A Portable Chaos* was the First Prize Winner of the Eric Hoffer Award for Fiction. But Schorb maintains that he is first and foremost a poet, and his poetry has appeared in numerous publications, here and abroad.

www.ingramcontent.com/pod-product-compliance
Lightning Source LLC
LaVergne TN
LVHW020100090426
835510LV00040B/2746